MATH PUZZLES FOR KIDS 2

Number Blocks
for Children

written by

Peter I. Kattan
and
Nicola I. Kattan

www.PetraBooks.com

www.PetraBooks.com

Ordering Information:
Quantity sales. Special discounts are available on quantity purchases by corporations, associations. Orders by U.S. trade bookstores and wholesalers. Please visit www.PetraBooks.com

Printed in the United States of America

ISBN-13: 979-8-8692-1054-8

Rules for Number Blocks

1. Fill in the missing **numbers** in each **block**.

2. The missing **numbers** are integers between **0 and 9**.

3. The **numbers** in each **row** add up to the totals on the right.

4. The **numbers** in each **column** add up to the totals on the bottom.

5. The diagonals also add up to the totals on the upper and lower right corners.

Math Puzzles for Kids 2
Number Blocks for Children

1
SUPER EASY

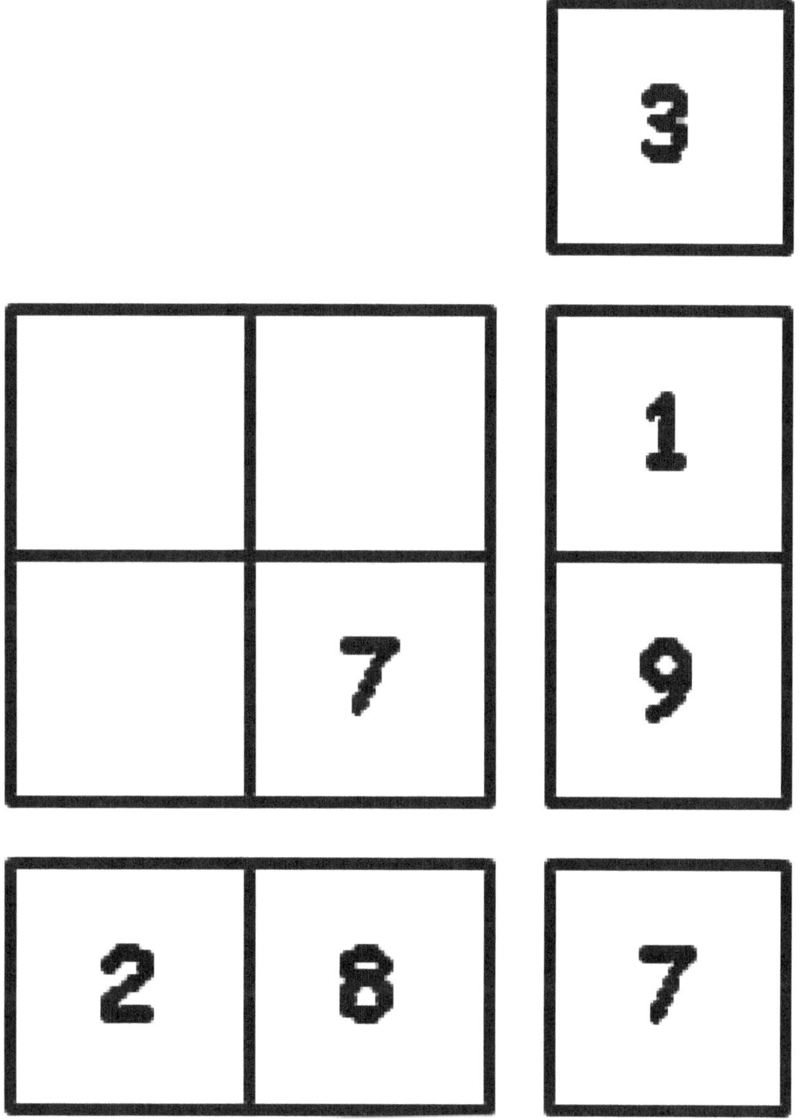

2
SUPER EASY

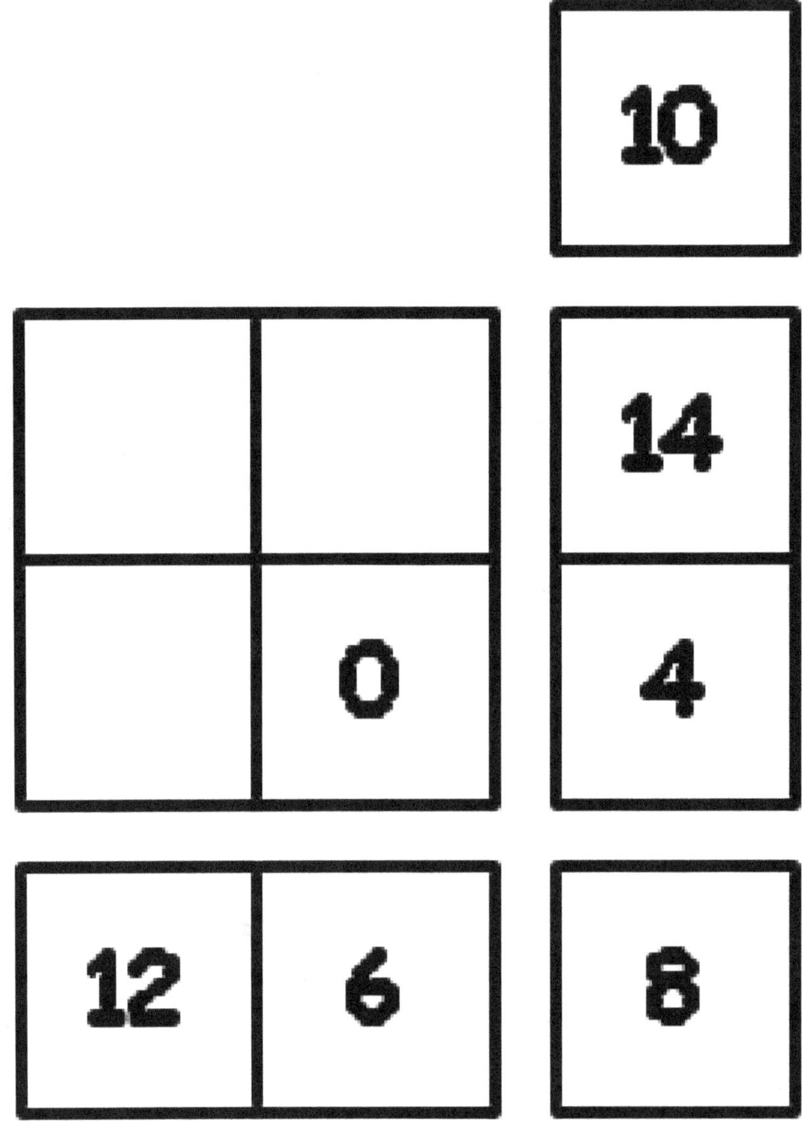

3
SUPER EASY

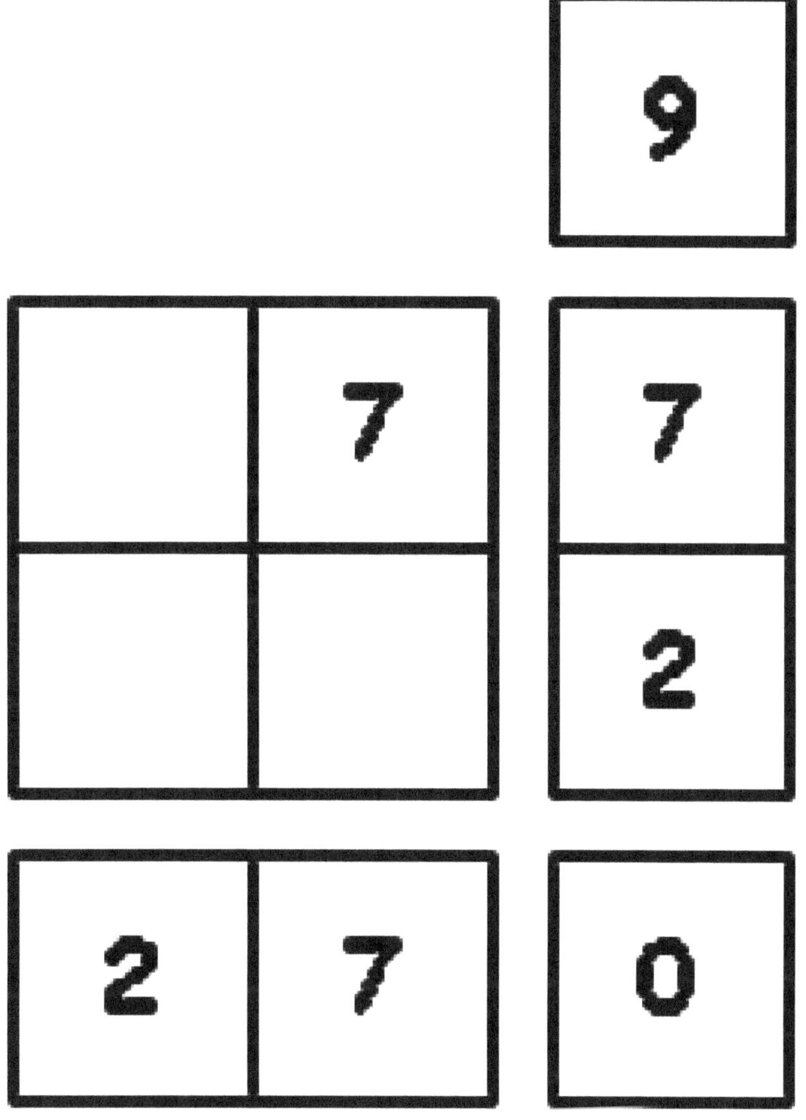

4
SUPER EASY

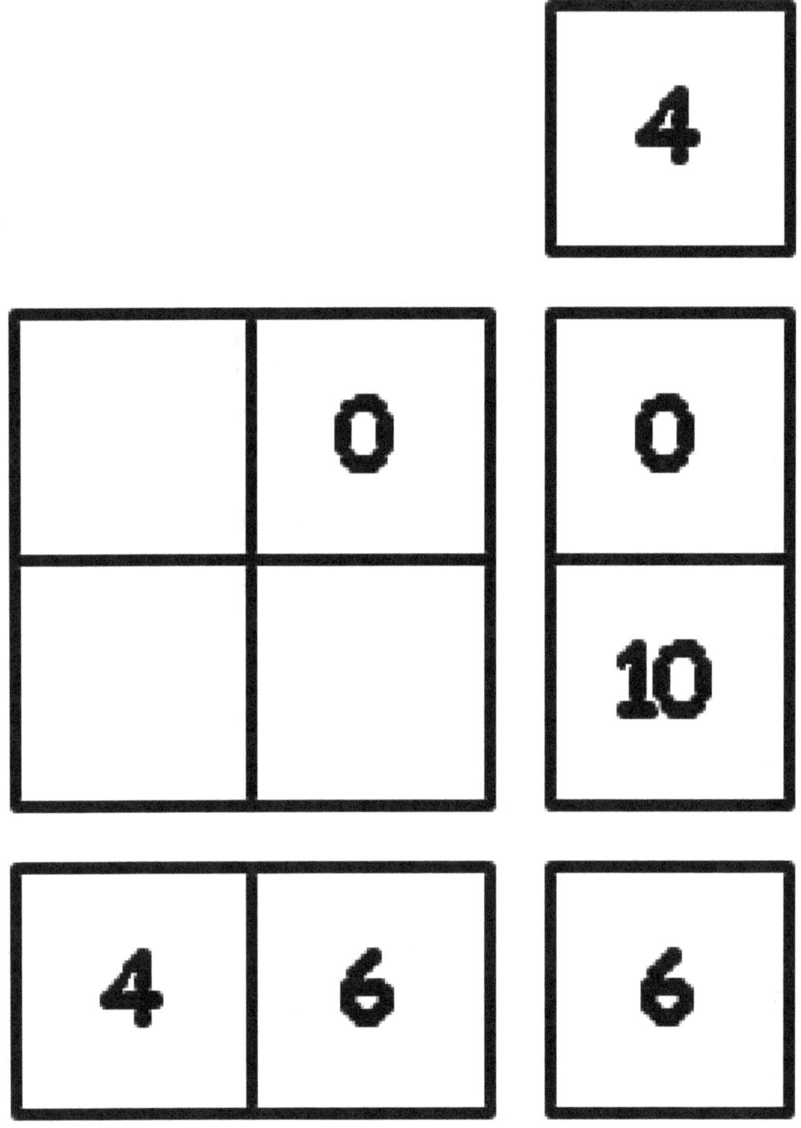

5
SUPER EASY

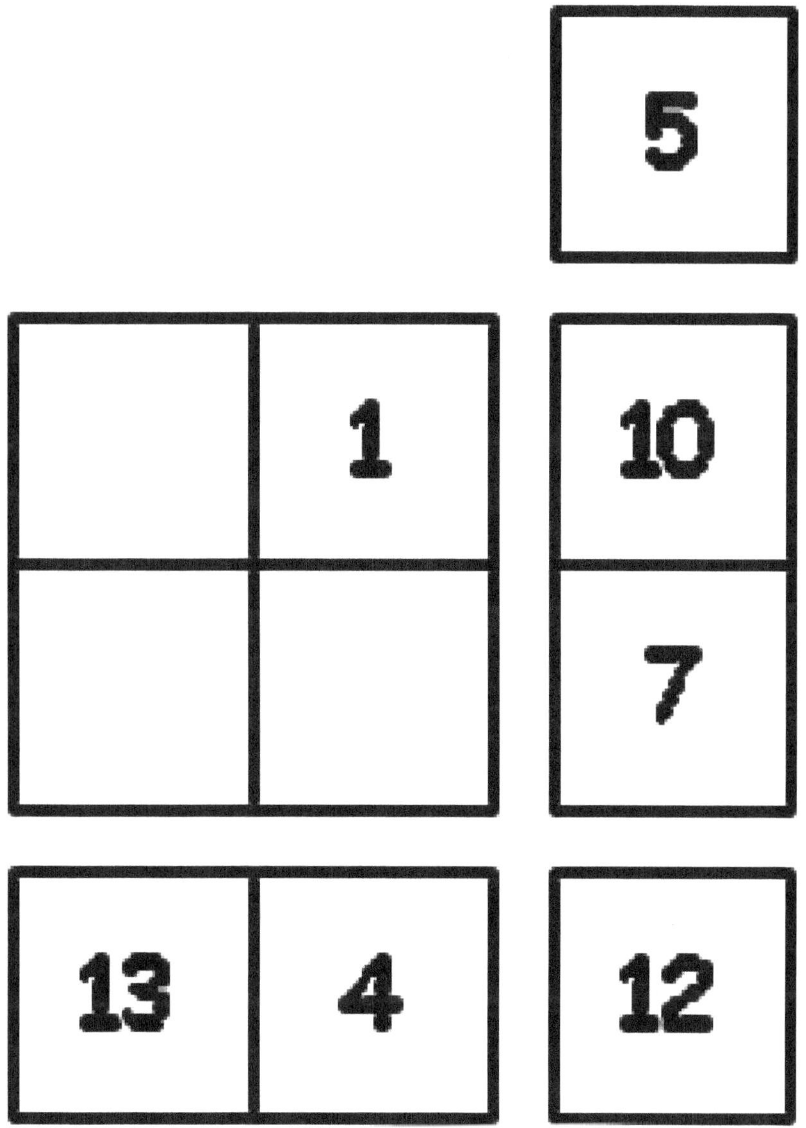

6
SUPER EASY

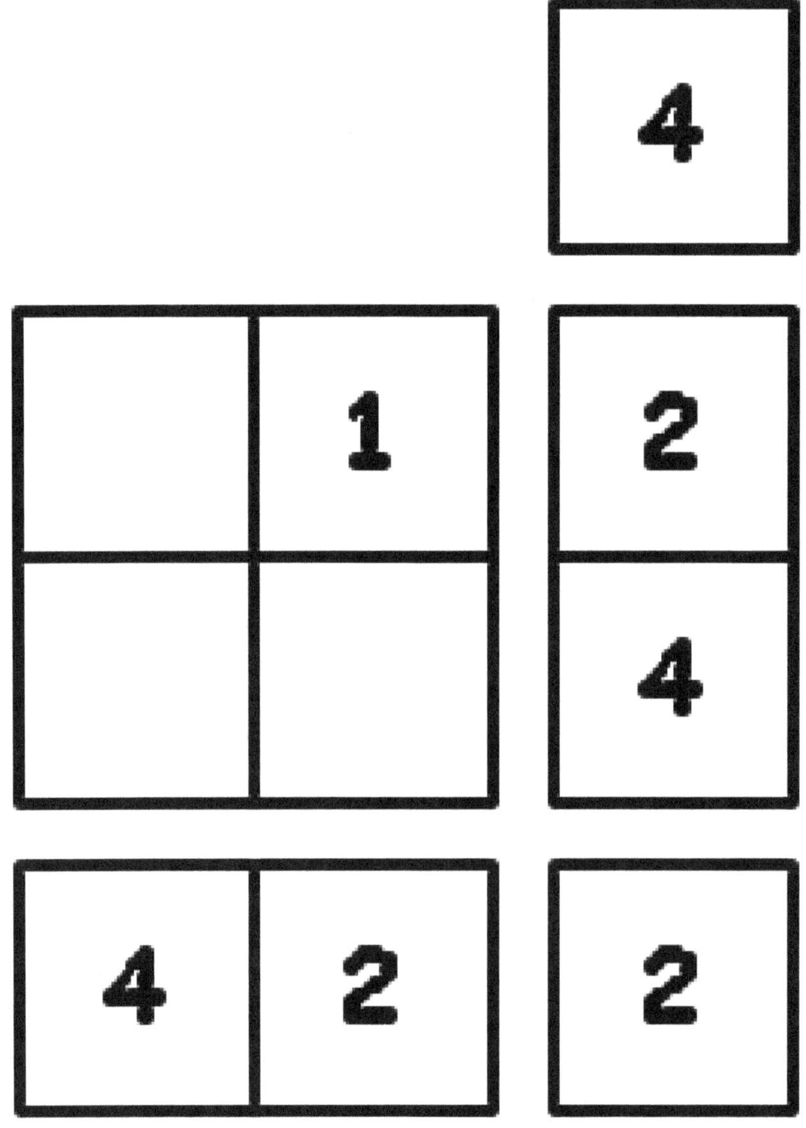

7
SUPER EASY

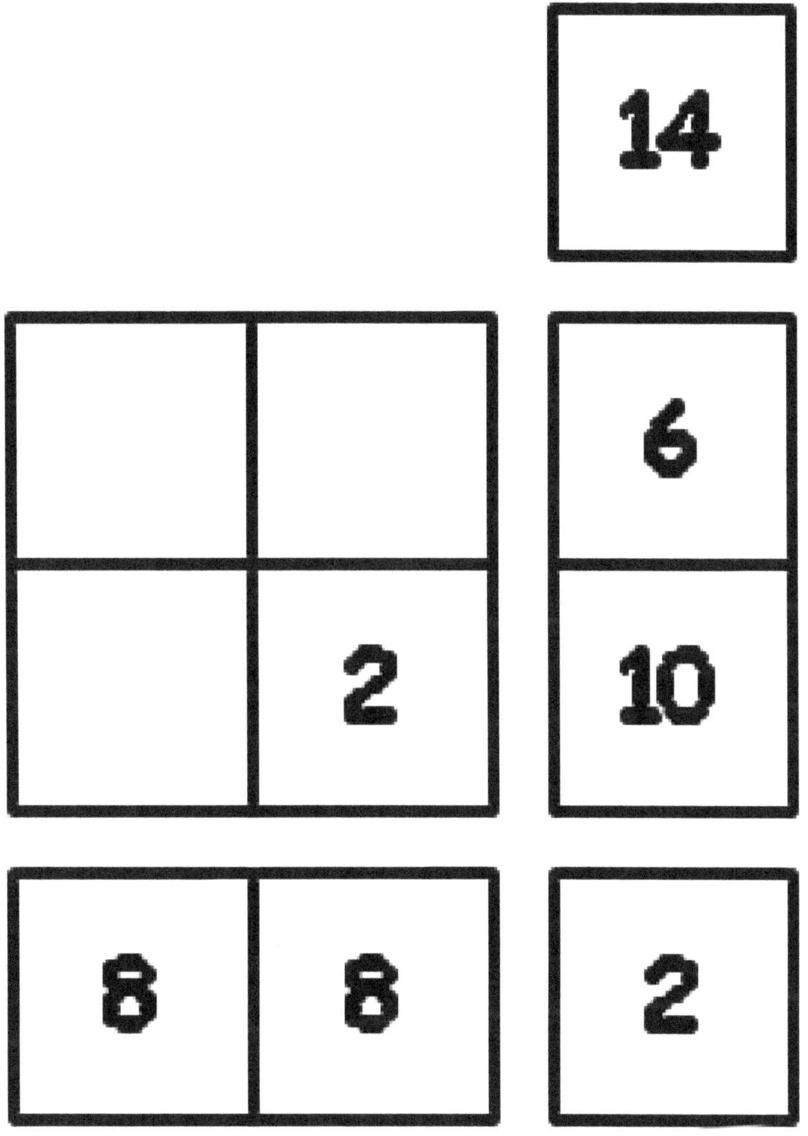

8
SUPER EASY

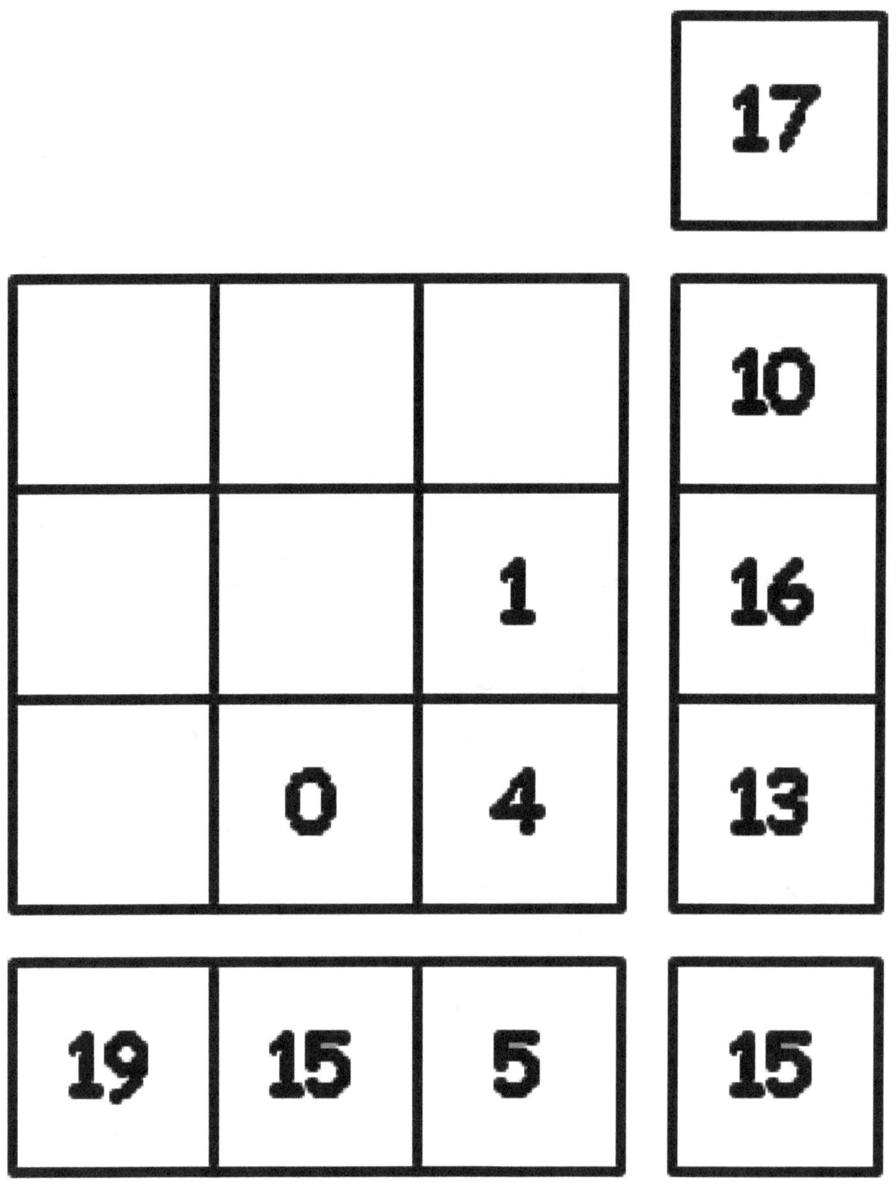

9
SUPER EASY

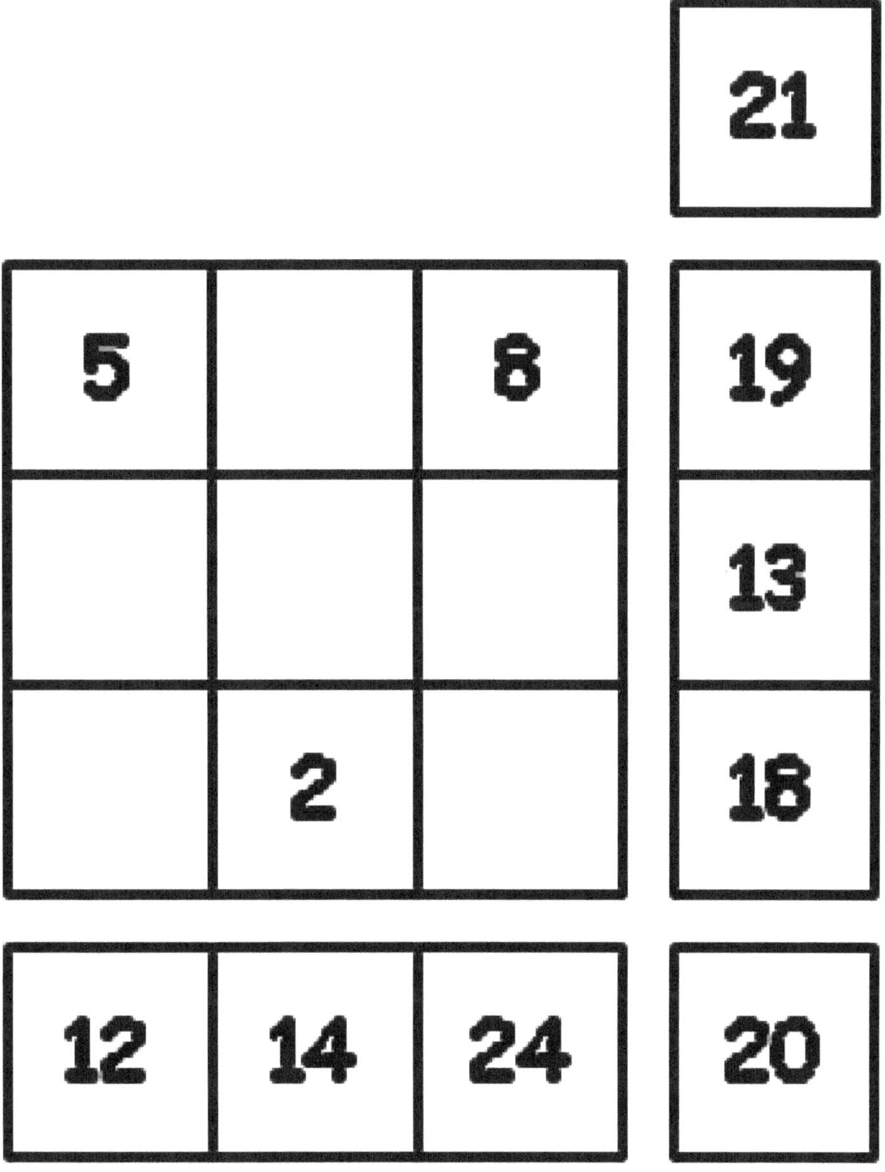

10
SUPER EASY

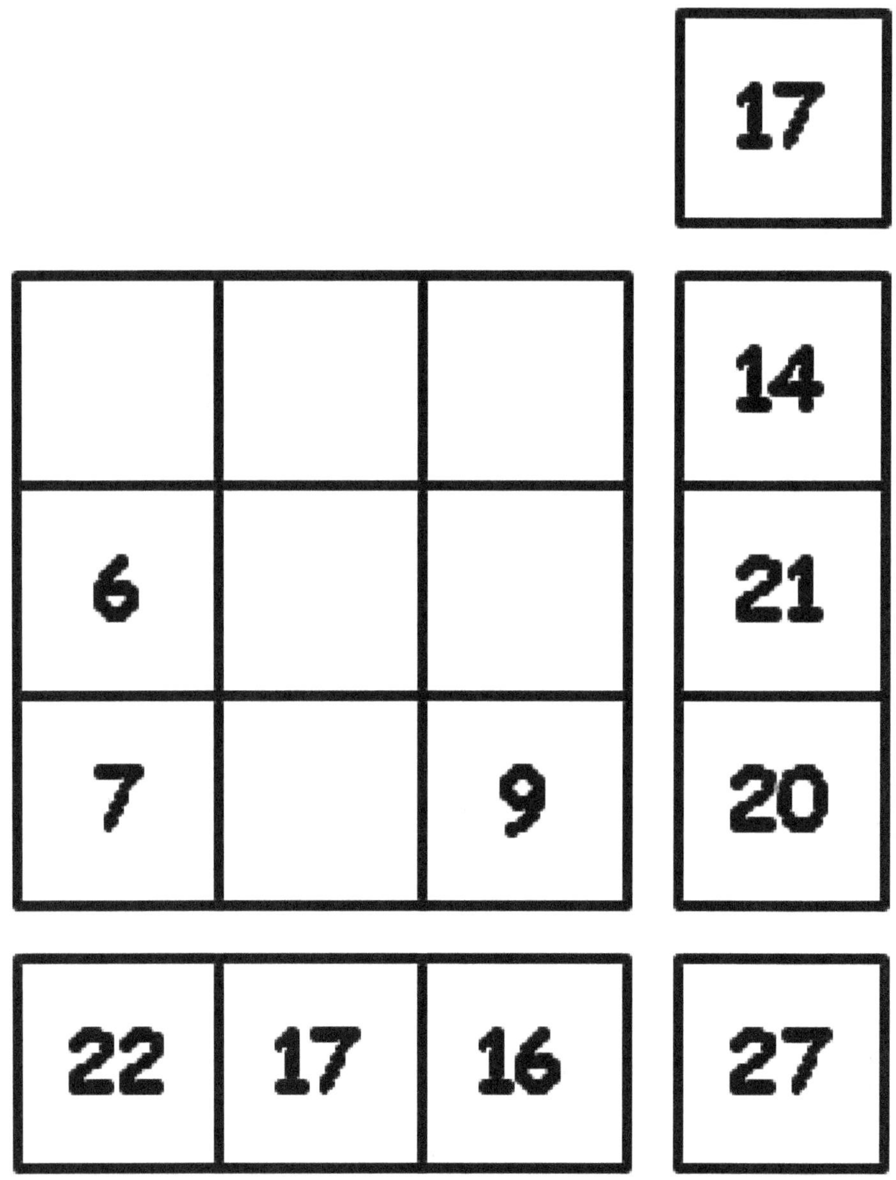

11
SUPER EASY

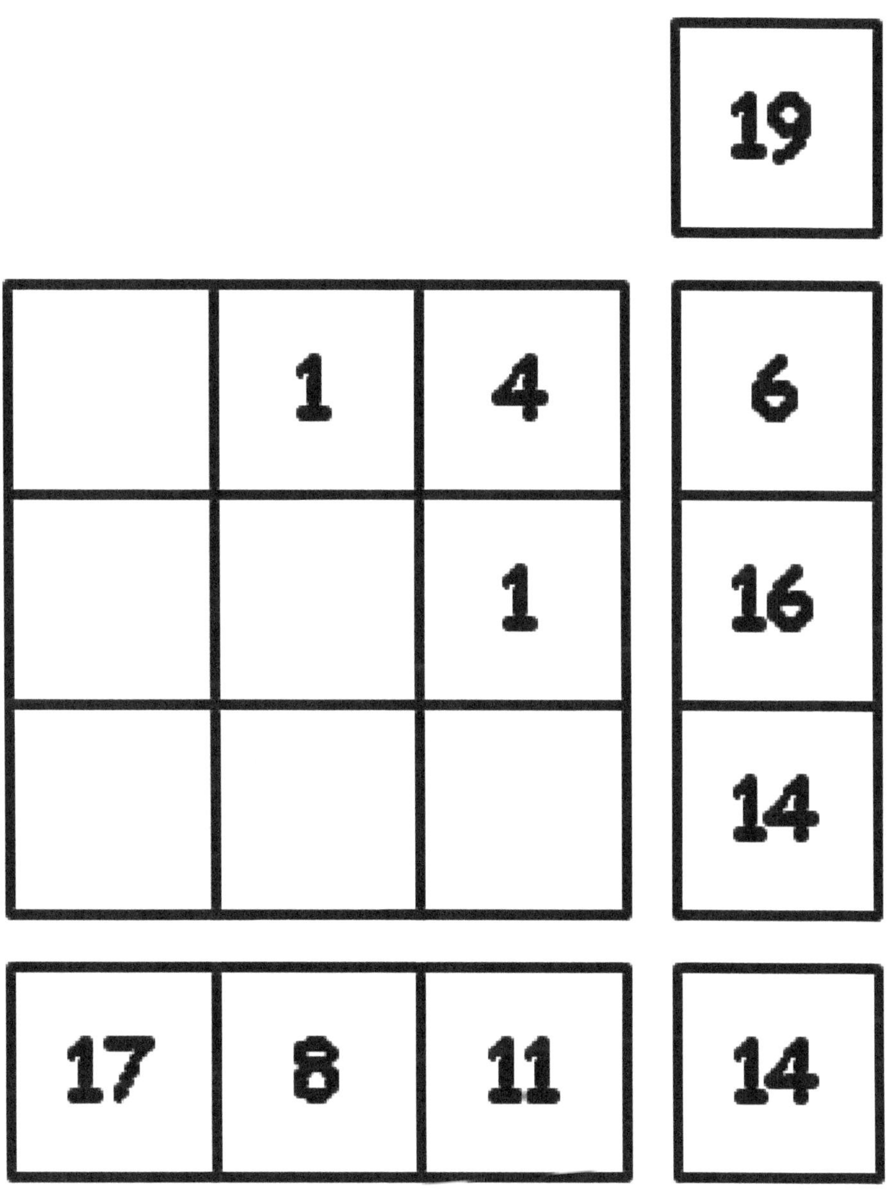

12
SUPER EASY

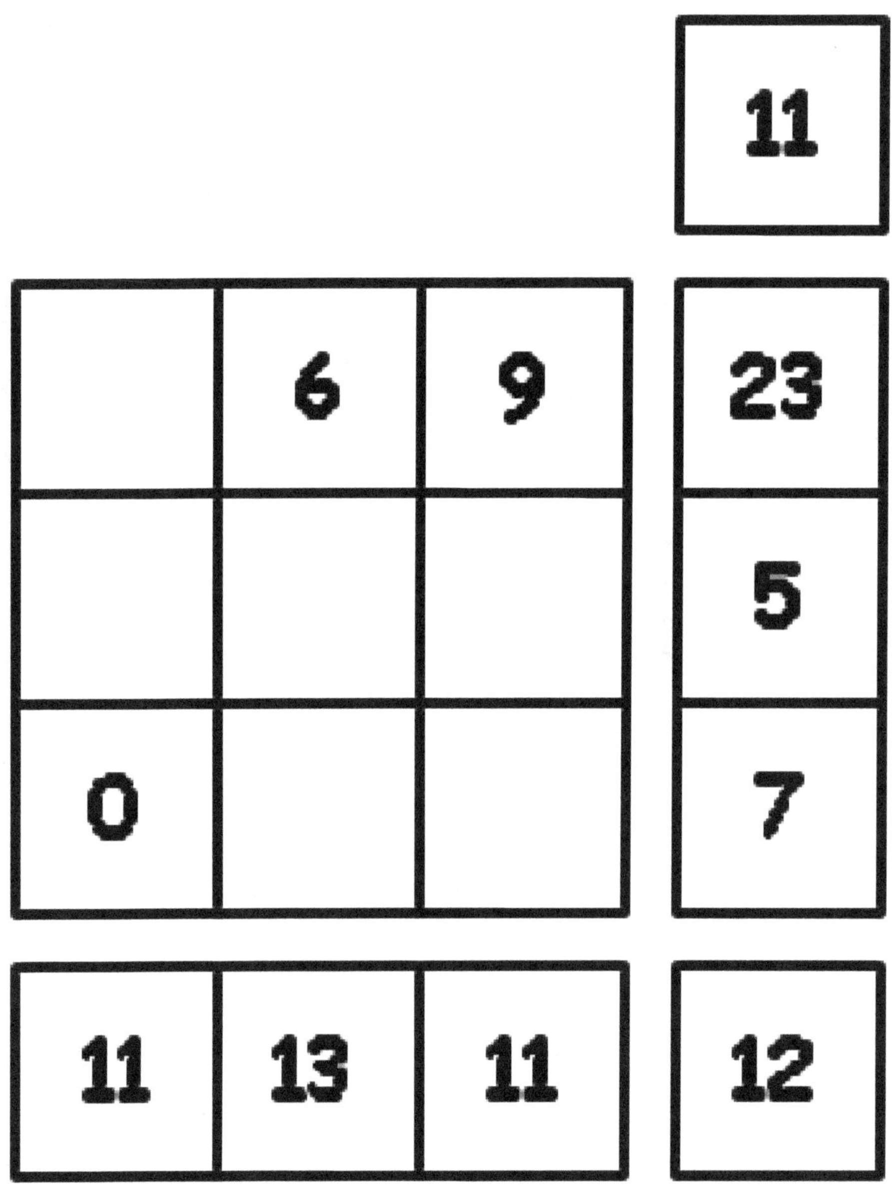

13
SUPER EASY

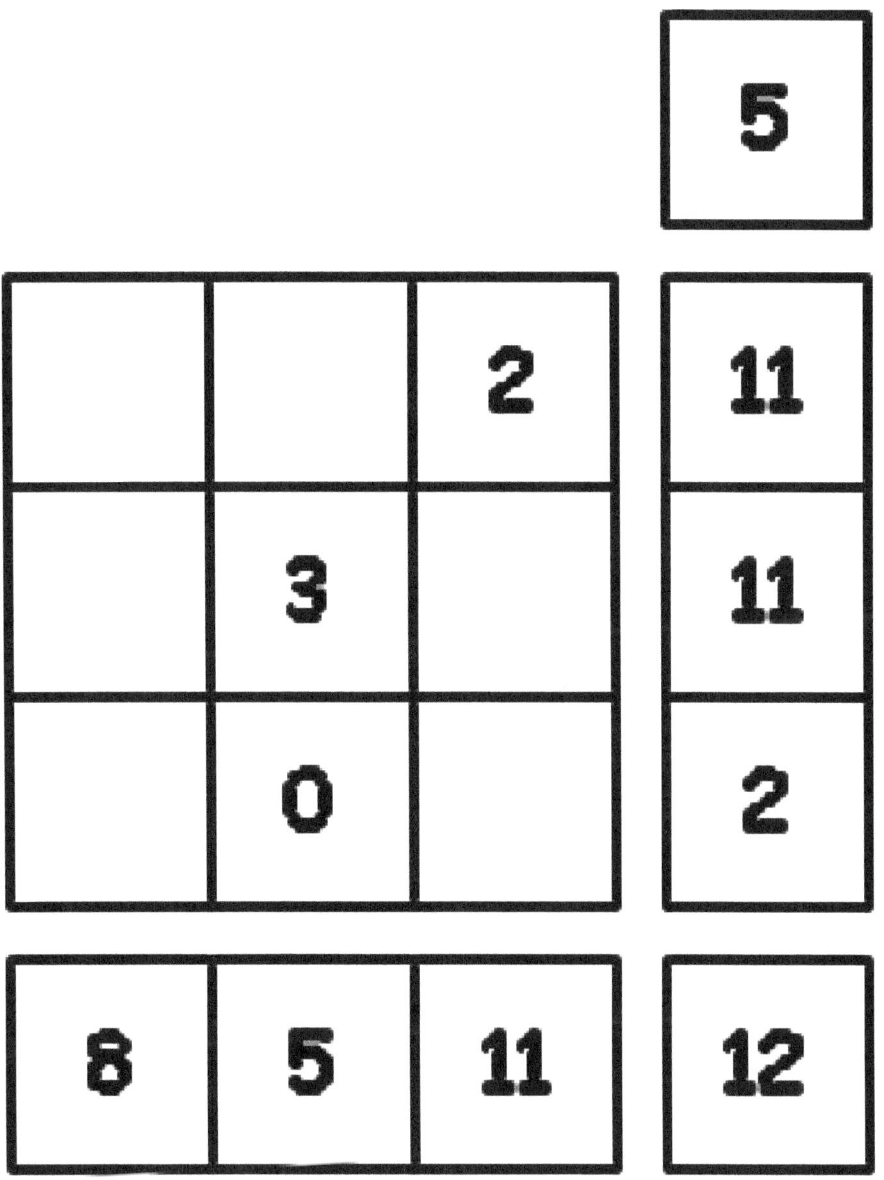

14
SUPER EASY

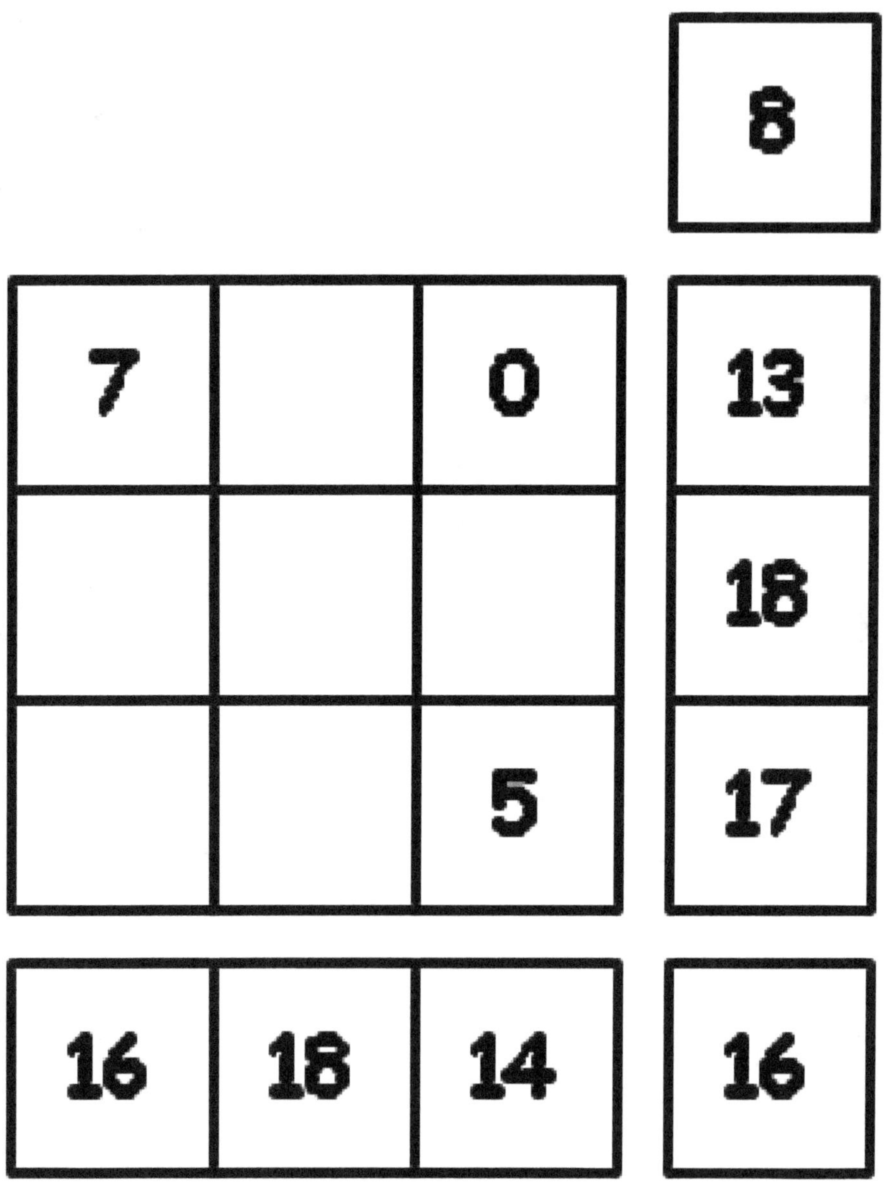

15
EASY

				14
				20
		4	7	**11**
	4			**11**
	3			**16**
4	**15**	**22**	**17**	**7**

16
EASY

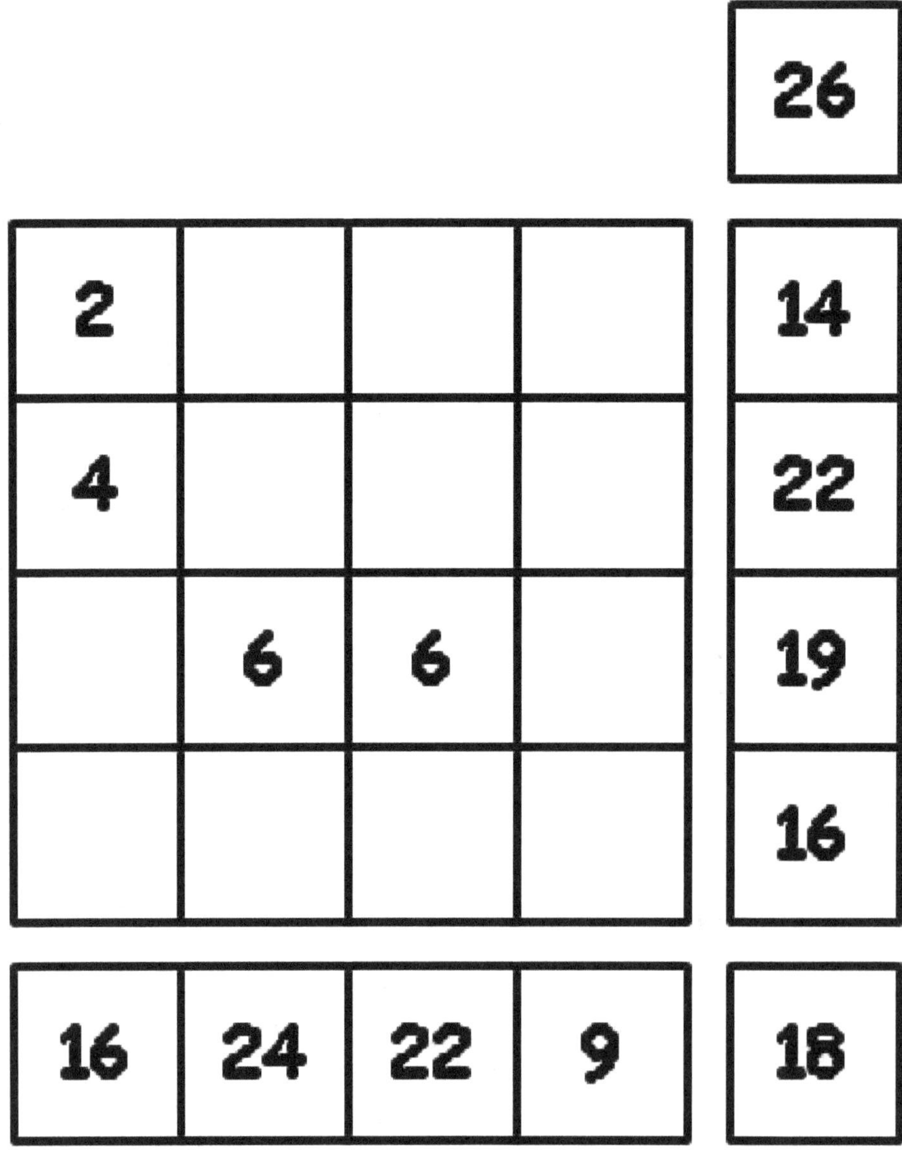

17
EASY

				17
		9	1	15
				23
	4			18
7				21
17	16	25	19	18

18
EASY

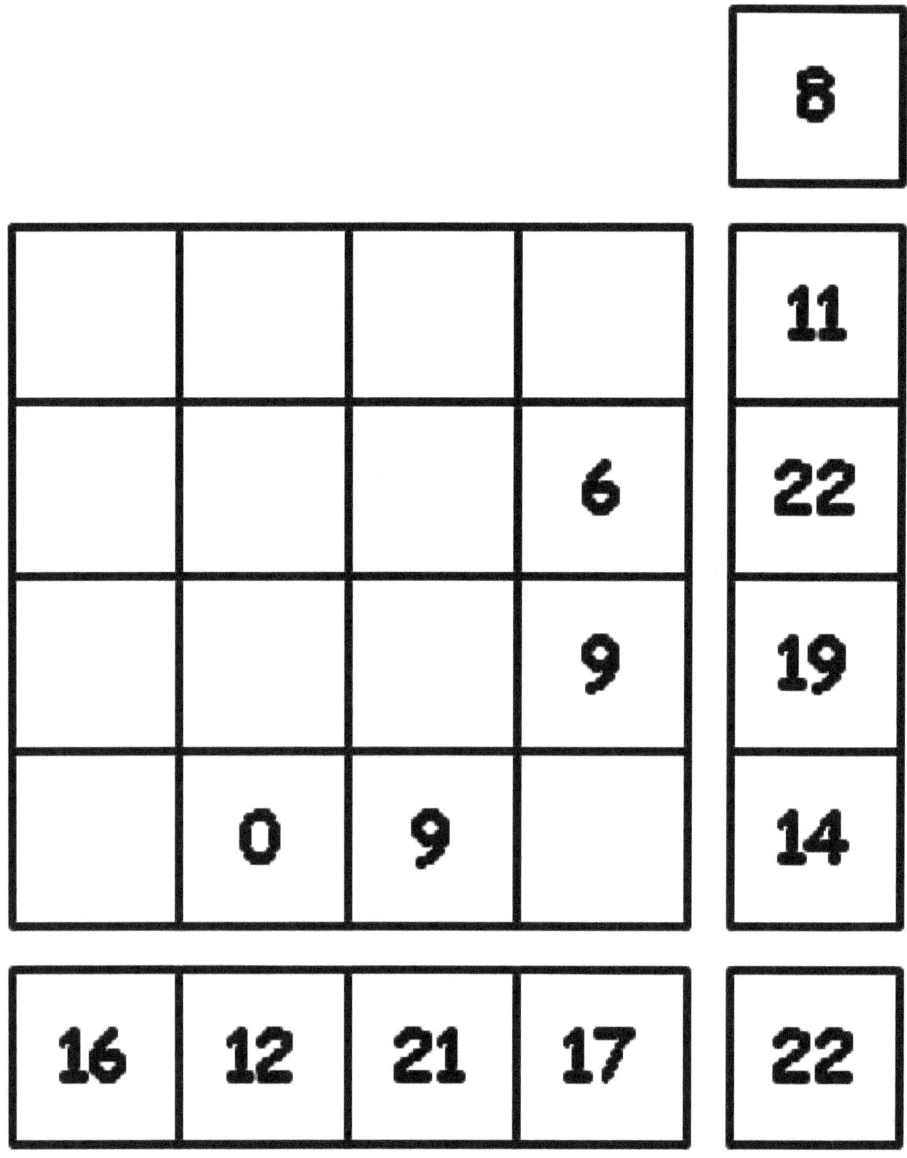

19
EASY

		3		**18**
			3	**25**
1			5	**14**
				11
				14

12	20	18	14	**13**

20
EASY

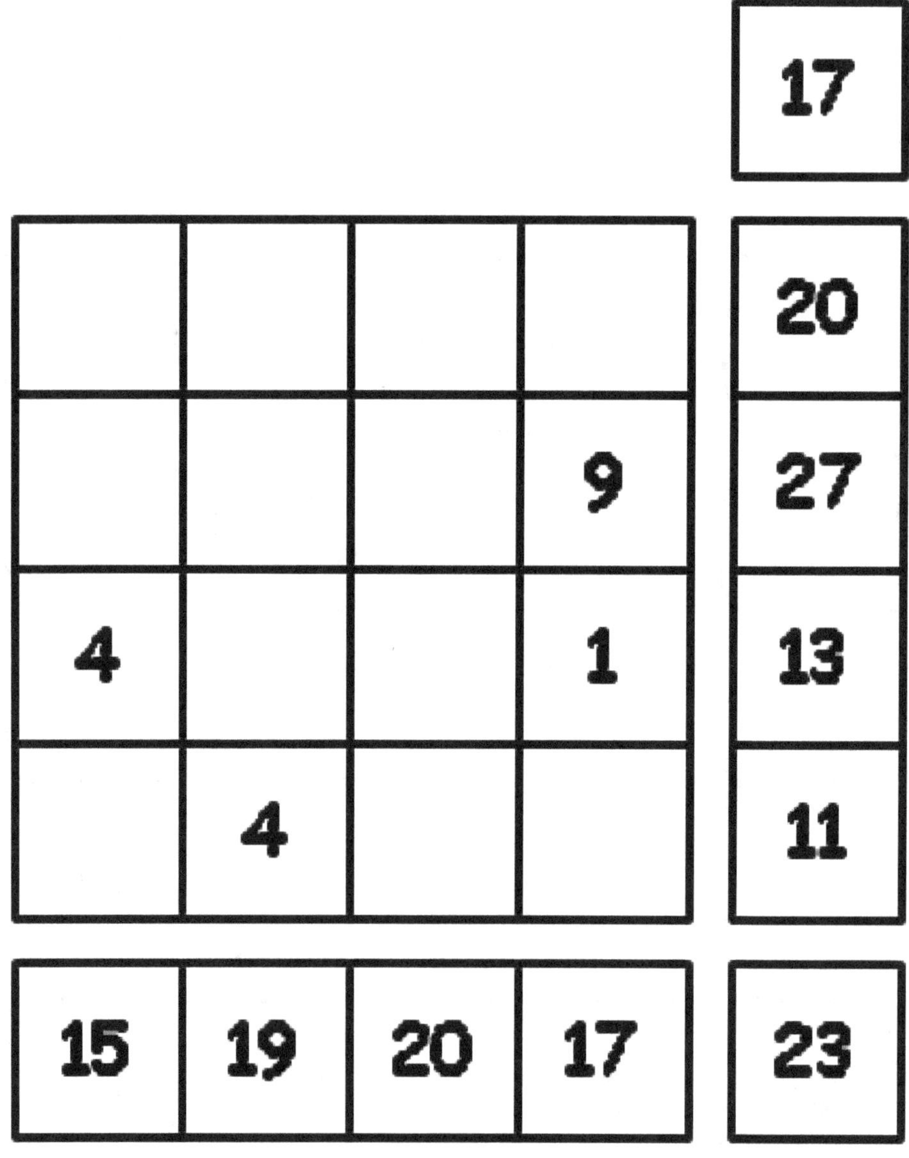

21
EASY

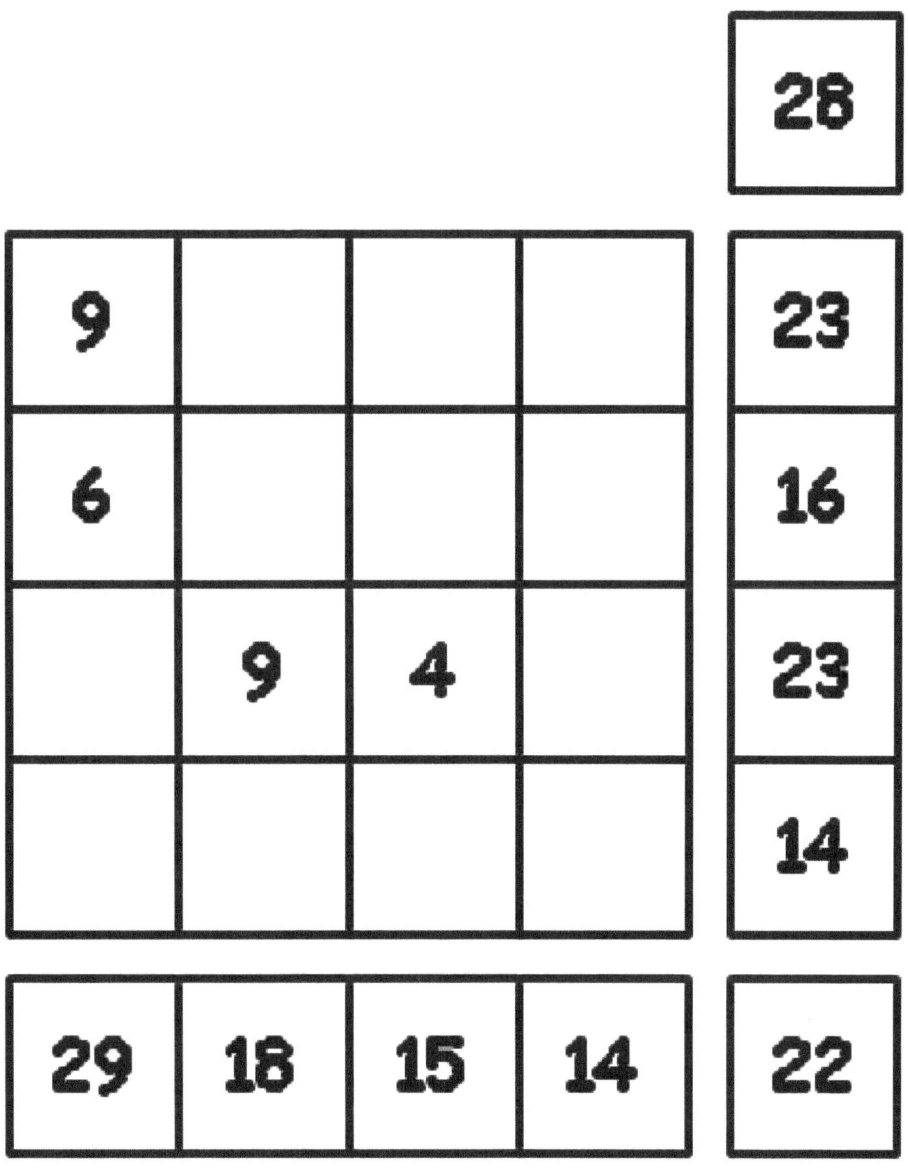

22
EASY - MEDIUM

					14
4	5				21
		4			17
					37
				7	28
	1	7	4		19
19	18	28	29	28	25

23
EASY - MEDIUM

<table>
<tr><td></td><td></td><td></td><td></td><td></td><td>31</td></tr>
<tr><td>5</td><td></td><td></td><td>6</td><td></td><td>21</td></tr>
<tr><td></td><td>7</td><td>5</td><td></td><td></td><td>30</td></tr>
<tr><td></td><td>8</td><td></td><td></td><td></td><td>29</td></tr>
<tr><td></td><td></td><td></td><td></td><td>9</td><td>38</td></tr>
<tr><td></td><td></td><td></td><td></td><td>2</td><td>18</td></tr>
<tr><td>20</td><td>27</td><td>34</td><td>28</td><td>27</td><td>31</td></tr>
</table>

24
EASY - MEDIUM

		0		1	**14**
2		7			19
					31
					16
			9		27
0				8	23
22	17	19	35	23	36

25
EASY - MEDIUM

					21
	6				24
6			6		26
3	6				23
		1			15
			7		26
19	28	19	30	18	23

26
EASY - MEDIUM

					31
		9			21
			9		33
2	8				32
2		5		2	21
					27
18	27	33	31	25	32

27
EASY - MEDIUM

						20
						18
4	7	4	2			19
	0			4		14
						27
		7				31

| 8 | 21 | 29 | 31 | 20 | | 25 |

28
EASY - MEDIUM

					23
5	**5**		**6**		**28**
					23
0	**7**				**13**
			0		**22**
	8				**24**

20	**31**	**23**	**17**	**19**	**20**

29
MEDIUM

8					6
		8		4	
8					
	1			8	
		2		4	

| 25 |
| 30 |
| 26 |
| 32 |
| 35 |
| 23 |
| 22 |

36	17	43	21	24	27	42

30
MEDIUM

						24
			0			10
0			9			33
		4				22
6			0		2	26
	0	3				20
						30
17	17	28	26	26	27	11

31
MEDIUM

						16
	0					23
		6				36
				2	0	12
				0		14
			0		1	18
			6	5		41
28	18	31	26	24	17	24

32
MEDIUM

<table>
<tr><td></td><td></td><td></td><td></td><td></td><td></td><td>25</td></tr>
<tr><td></td><td></td><td></td><td></td><td></td><td></td><td>25</td></tr>
<tr><td></td><td></td><td></td><td></td><td>1</td><td></td><td>28</td></tr>
<tr><td></td><td>5</td><td></td><td>5</td><td></td><td>4</td><td>29</td></tr>
<tr><td></td><td></td><td></td><td></td><td>2</td><td>8</td><td>20</td></tr>
<tr><td></td><td>7</td><td></td><td>5</td><td></td><td></td><td>44</td></tr>
<tr><td>3</td><td></td><td></td><td></td><td></td><td></td><td>20</td></tr>
<tr><td>31</td><td>26</td><td>27</td><td>28</td><td>23</td><td>31</td><td>24</td></tr>
</table>

33
MEDIUM

							25
	7			9			26
				1			24
			5	5			16
			5				28
	3	0					21
8							29
22	29	13	27	21	32		16

34
MEDIUM

<table>
<tr><td></td><td>3</td><td></td><td></td><td>0</td><td></td><td>19</td></tr>
<tr><td></td><td></td><td></td><td></td><td></td><td>1</td><td>29</td></tr>
<tr><td></td><td>2</td><td></td><td></td><td></td><td></td><td>33</td></tr>
<tr><td></td><td></td><td>3</td><td></td><td>1</td><td>1</td><td>13</td></tr>
<tr><td>7</td><td></td><td></td><td></td><td></td><td></td><td>28</td></tr>
<tr><td></td><td>5</td><td></td><td></td><td></td><td></td><td>33</td></tr>
<tr><td>28</td><td>21</td><td>28</td><td>42</td><td>16</td><td>20</td><td>31</td></tr>
</table>

27

35
MEDIUM

							28
		1					23
							35
			5	7	0		23
			7				22
2		4	5				27
			7				33
27	23	19	33	32	29		39

36
MEDIUM - DIFFICULT

					6		**34**
9		8					**30**
	8		7				**43**
	6	0				5	**33**
1		9			7	9	**18**
			6				**37**
6							**43**
							28
33	**42**	**36**	**27**	**22**	**26**	**46**	**31**

37
MEDIUM - DIFFICULT

							41
							34
					5		**31**
9						4	**53**
	1		9			8	**28**
		1	9	0		7	**25**
8	7						**43**
	0				4		**30**
32	**36**	**36**	**39**	**28**	**30**	**43**	**44**

38
MEDIUM - DIFFICULT

<table>
<tr><td></td><td>8</td><td></td><td></td><td>7</td><td></td><td></td><td>25</td></tr>
<tr><td></td><td>5</td><td></td><td></td><td></td><td>3</td><td></td><td>27</td></tr>
<tr><td></td><td></td><td></td><td>1</td><td></td><td></td><td>2</td><td>30</td></tr>
<tr><td>9</td><td></td><td></td><td></td><td></td><td>3</td><td></td><td>32</td></tr>
<tr><td></td><td></td><td></td><td>6</td><td>4</td><td></td><td>6</td><td>33</td></tr>
<tr><td></td><td></td><td>6</td><td>4</td><td></td><td></td><td></td><td>41</td></tr>
<tr><td></td><td></td><td></td><td></td><td></td><td></td><td>4</td><td>27</td></tr>
<tr><td></td><td></td><td></td><td></td><td></td><td></td><td></td><td>18</td></tr>
<tr><td>33</td><td>35</td><td>43</td><td>17</td><td>20</td><td>23</td><td>37</td><td>14</td></tr>
</table>

39
MEDIUM - DIFFICULT

							24
			7			0	17
	0						36
							26
	0		0	3		6	21
9					8		42
		9		4		6	37
	0				9		36
34	8	39	32	26	40	36	21

40
MEDIUM - DIFFICULT

							35
		0		5	8		34
							36
		4	1				26
	3				9		23
				2	5		31
	2	6					29
6	7					2	33
29	26	32	33	31	38	23	29

41
MEDIUM - DIFFICULT

								12
1								22
					0	6		17
		3	1					20
0	7							28
1		0						33
1						7		34
		8	5			4		39
22	30	19	30	25	34	33		26

42
MEDIUM - DIFFICULT

<table>
<tr><td></td><td></td><td></td><td></td><td>8</td><td></td><td>8</td><td>40</td></tr>
<tr><td></td><td></td><td></td><td></td><td></td><td></td><td></td><td>43</td></tr>
<tr><td></td><td></td><td></td><td></td><td></td><td></td><td></td><td>30</td></tr>
<tr><td>5</td><td></td><td>1</td><td></td><td></td><td>2</td><td></td><td>28</td></tr>
<tr><td>7</td><td></td><td>9</td><td></td><td>3</td><td></td><td>6</td><td>32</td></tr>
<tr><td></td><td></td><td></td><td></td><td></td><td>4</td><td></td><td>40</td></tr>
<tr><td></td><td></td><td></td><td></td><td>7</td><td></td><td></td><td>36</td></tr>
<tr><td></td><td></td><td></td><td>1</td><td>2</td><td></td><td>9</td><td>39</td></tr>
<tr><td>32</td><td>34</td><td>47</td><td>20</td><td>35</td><td>30</td><td>50</td><td>26</td></tr>
</table>

43
DIFFICULT

								38
4		8	4					30
			3					49
	7					7	5	54
		0	2		9			44
	9							47
			5	4			0	43
5	4	8		4			8	43
							1	27
49	41	38	29	44	53	47	36	35

44
DIFFICULT

								24
			9	0				38
5	5			5		3		39
						3		44
	5					8	5	37
1		3	1					30
5		7	1					29
	0			2	4			26
							8	52
33	34	41	50	28	42	37	30	36

45
DIFFICULT

								26
	3	5			4			**35**
	1			5				**35**
								33
		3		1		6		**38**
8	8			6	8			**53**
	8		7				2	**45**
					9	8		**46**
7		5					5	**45**
52	**31**	**38**	**42**	**40**	**48**	**43**	**36**	**39**

46
DIFFICULT

									22
									36
	8			9					42
9	2	3							23
7	0					2			39
		6		4					37
	6					1	8		38
5				7		7			39
1	9		2			9			34
34	43	40	35	39	35	39	23		40

47
DIFFICULT

								36
		1			1		1	13
	1							33
		9	4		2			37
	6		4	6				35
			1			2		21
		4						39
0		4		7			7	26
					8	1	2	33
43	31	27	32	39	22	24	19	30

48
DIFFICULT

								42
				8		5	8	48
				7	9		9	54
	2		0		4			21
4	4	6		7				32
								31
					8			40
1			4		4	4		40
		2			2			30
33	26	32	36	50	37	42	40	46

49
DIFFICULT

14

								30
4	7							41
		6		4				36
	2	4						32
				0	3	0		51
		7	3	8	7			39
		4		9		1	7	33
9	1						7	32

41	37	34	31	45	40	21	45	36

50
SUPER - DIFFICULT

										45
1										45
			2					2		39
9	7		9		2					50
		8	2				2			48
	8			4			9			49
8		8				9				39
6										30
		2	7	6						35
		3		7	6	9		6		41
43	43	47	29	28	32	64	50	40		30

51
SUPER - DIFFICULT

									39
0		4						4	**50**
									34
			7		2		9	0	**48**
		0	1					2	**40**
	1	1							**22**
					8		3		**47**
				7			0	6	**39**
1			2		6				**33**
5	0		4	8			1		**36**
30	**38**	**24**	**35**	**46**	**44**	**65**	**39**	**28**	**36**

52
SUPER - DIFFICULT

									33
	3						0	2	25
	8						7		48
		4						5	23
	4	7		2	3	1		0	33
			6				8		55
	9		7			9			53
4				8			9		54
	1				7			2	37
							3		43
38	49	36	35	42	50	39	37	45	39

53
SUPER - DIFFICULT

									36
		7					7	6	**53**
				2		1		0	**25**
	8					3			**40**
		6		7	1	8			**40**
				6		2	0		**35**
					4		8		**40**
		3			3	4			**45**
6	9	3						9	**45**
								9	**36**
50	**60**	**27**	**37**	**43**	**23**	**29**	**50**	**40**	**46**

54
SUPER - DIFFICULT

	2		6		5				36
			5	3					32
5		1	7				6		40
			0	7			4	6	38
		1	1					6	43
7	9						6		38
				8					48
	3	6						0	31
7	4								35
									45
45	38	33	45	37	41	31	37	43	23

55
SUPER - DIFFICULT

									45
			6		5	1			41
		6			9			8	46
		9				4			46
				8			3	2	38
7									36
4		1		7			8		46
	1		0						29
2		4		2			4		42
				9	0	7			39
30	36	33	41	49	47	34	43	50	38

56
SUPER - DIFFICULT

									42
2					1			0	37
	9						5		55
	4			1		6			36
	8			5	3	0			39
0					7				49
4							8		39
						0	4	4	38
		0	2	0					24
			2		6		9		52
37	56	51	39	24	32	45	51	34	37

57
SUPER - DIFFICULT

										47
				4				1		40
		8			6	2		9	7	54
								1	0	23
5		2			7					53
				4		7		8		59
9	3				4		6			47
5			0	8	6	4		0		41
	3				1		8			35
		6			4		9	3		48
	7		6						3	47
51	47	39	45	32	50	41	56	49	37	**55**

58
SUPER - DIFFICULT

										27
	6			4		6		3		**42**
	4	1								**33**
	7	4	7		9		3			**46**
5				5	3			3		**43**
		6								**51**
0	3				5	1	9			**31**
	1		2		1			0	1	**31**
					3		1			**33**
				4			3		0	**40**
0			4			4		9		**38**
48	**37**	**41**	**45**	**45**	**25**	**41**	**41**	**38**	**27**	**42**

59
SUPER - DIFFICULT

											31
											56
						7			2		33
	1		0								52
5			2		7	0	6				46
					2	6	9				44
	3				3						52
	8			8		2	2	4	5		52
	7	1	8		2	5		7	7		53
				4	2				4		44
	6	6	7	2		6					50
40	53	39	42	45	52	53	60	48	50		41

60
SUPER - DIFFICULT

										50
	1	0	1	6		2	3		2	29
8	4		9							51
8		3	7							48
	1	3			9					33
			8					4	5	54
	3			8			5	6	3	51
									7	43
				0			5	4		44
	9					9				65
	2	3	6	4					6	49
51	41	37	47	52	42	42	50	51	54	48

61
SUPER - DIFFICULT

										56
1	2						9	6		47
			3		9	2	4	5		50
5					9			0	4	50
	8					9	9			62
7								3		46
	7	1				6			1	34
	3							5		41
	7		4			6	0			41
							7	2	8	65
9	0			7					4	37
58	51	32	30	57	46	58	53	40	48	32

62
SUPER - DIFFICULT

										38
							2			41
2						6		4	7	45
2		3	4		2		1			25
				0					2	40
8	8					7	4	7		62
8						8		0		62
4		8				9	0	8		45
9			5		2				1	41
	3									48
	6			6	1			9	2	44
54	58	44	54	35	20	59	43	50	36	51

63
SUPER - DIFFICULT

										50
2				2		5				35
	7	8			0	0	6			43
				8		1		1		41
5						1		4		39
	9	3		2	3		8			42
		3			0		3	5		49
	1		3						4	37
							1		2	40
			5			6	2	6		51
			7		2		1			51
46	63	36	47	50	31	25	32	38	60	29

1

		3
0	1	1
2	7	9
2	8	7

2

		10
8	6	14
4	0	4
12	6	8

SOLUTIONS

3

		9
0	7	7
2	0	2
2	7	0

4

		4
0	0	0
4	6	10
4	6	6

5

		5

9	1	10
4	3	7

13	4	12

6

		4

1	1	2
3	1	4

4	2	2

SOLUTIONS

7

		14

0	6	6
8	2	10

8	8	2

8

			17

3	7	0	10
7	8	1	16
9	0	4	13

19	15	5	15

9

			21
5	6	8	19
0	6	7	13
7	2	9	18
12	14	24	20

10

			17
9	4	1	14
6	9	6	21
7	4	9	20
22	17	16	27

SOLUTIONS

11

			19
1	1	4	6
8	7	1	16
8	0	6	14
17	8	11	14

12

			11
8	6	9	23
3	2	0	5
0	5	2	7
11	13	11	12

13

			5
7	2	2	11
1	3	7	11
0	0	2	2
8	5	11	12

14

			8
7	6	0	13
5	4	9	18
4	8	5	17
16	18	14	16

SOLUTIONS

15

				14
0	8	9	3	20
0	0	4	7	11
1	4	3	3	11
3	3	6	4	16
4	15	22	17	7

16

				26
2	4	0	8	14
4	9	9	0	22
7	6	6	0	19
3	5	7	1	16
16	24	22	9	18

17

				17
5	0	9	1	15
2	7	5	9	23
3	4	4	7	18
7	5	7	2	21
17	16	25	19	18

18

				8
4	2	3	2	11
7	9	0	6	22
0	1	9	9	19
5	0	9	0	14
16	12	21	17	22

SOLUTIONS

19

				18
9	7	3	6	25
1	4	6	3	14
1	5	0	5	11
1	4	9	0	14
12	20	18	14	13

20

				17
6	7	3	4	20
2	7	9	9	27
4	1	7	1	13
3	4	1	3	11
15	19	20	17	23

21

				28
9	3	3	8	23
6	5	5	0	16
8	9	4	2	23
6	1	3	4	14
29	18	15	14	22

22

					14
4	5	8	1	3	21
3	2	4	6	2	17
8	8	3	9	9	37
4	2	6	9	7	28
0	1	7	4	7	19
19	18	28	29	28	25

SOLUTIONS

23

					31
5	3	5	6	2	21
1	7	5	9	8	30
1	8	9	5	6	29
7	5	9	8	9	38
6	4	6	0	2	18
20	27	34	28	27	31

24

					14
9	3	0	6	1	19
2	7	7	9	6	31
2	3	3	2	6	16
9	1	6	9	2	27
0	3	3	9	8	23
22	17	19	35	23	36

SOLUTIONS

25

					21
0	6	7	6	5	24
6	9	3	6	2	26
3	6	4	9	1	23
7	3	1	2	2	15
3	4	4	7	8	26
19	26	19	30	18	23

26

					31
3	3	9	5	1	21
3	8	4	9	9	33
2	8	9	4	9	32
2	4	5	8	2	21
8	4	6	5	4	27
18	27	33	31	25	32

27

					20
0	1	7	5	5	18
4	7	4	2	2	19
0	0	2	8	4	14
1	8	9	8	1	27
3	5	7	8	8	31
8	21	29	31	20	25

28

					23
5	5	6	6	6	28
4	6	3	3	7	23
0	7	5	0	1	13
7	5	9	0	1	22
4	8	0	8	4	24
20	31	23	17	19	20

SOLUTIONS

29

						25
8	1	8	3	4	6	30
8	2	7	7	1	1	26
5	8	8	1	4	6	32
8	4	9	8	3	3	35
0	1	9	2	8	3	23
7	1	2	0	4	8	22
36	17	43	21	24	27	42

30

						24
0	0	6	0	0	4	10
0	7	2	9	6	9	33
3	2	4	1	8	4	22
6	5	7	0	6	2	26
2	0	3	7	0	8	20
6	3	6	9	6	0	30
17	17	28	26	26	27	11

31

						16
3	0	8	7	5	0	23
6	1	6	8	9	6	36
1	5	4	0	2	0	12
4	3	0	5	0	2	14
8	1	5	0	3	1	18
6	8	8	6	5	8	41
28	18	31	26	24	17	24

32

						25
6	7	7	2	1	2	25
9	2	0	9	1	7	28
4	5	4	5	7	4	29
0	3	7	0	2	8	20
9	7	9	5	8	6	44
3	2	0	7	4	4	20
31	26	27	28	23	31	24

33

						25
2	7	2	3	9	3	26
4	2	5	4	1	8	24
2	2	0	5	5	2	16
4	8	5	5	1	5	28
2	3	0	7	1	8	21
8	7	1	3	4	6	29
22	29	13	27	21	32	16

34

						27
4	3	0	9	0	3	19
9	6	5	7	1	1	29
1	2	5	9	9	7	33
0	1	3	7	1	1	13
7	4	9	3	3	2	28
7	5	6	7	2	6	33
28	21	28	42	16	20	31

SOLUTIONS

35

						28
5	2	1	4	2	9	23
4	7	4	5	9	6	35
6	2	3	5	7	0	23
8	3	0	7	4	0	22
2	3	4	5	8	5	27
2	6	7	7	2	9	33
27	23	19	33	32	29	39

36

							34
1	4	6	6	1	6	6	30
9	9	8	5	2	5	5	43
4	8	4	7	1	0	9	33
3	6	0	0	4	0	5	18
1	1	9	3	7	7	9	37
9	7	8	6	1	5	7	43
6	7	1	0	6	3	5	28
33	42	36	27	22	26	46	31

37

							41
4	5	8	1	6	4	6	34
4	9	2	2	6	5	3	31
9	9	8	9	7	7	4	53
1	1	6	9	2	1	8	28
0	5	1	9	0	3	7	25
8	7	5	5	5	6	7	43
6	0	6	4	2	4	8	30
32	36	36	39	28	30	43	**44**

38

							25
0	8	8	0	7	0	4	27
3	5	9	3	1	3	6	30
6	9	0	1	6	8	2	32
9	4	8	0	0	3	9	33
9	3	7	6	4	6	6	41
5	4	6	4	1	1	6	27
1	2	5	3	1	2	4	18
33	35	43	17	20	23	37	**14**

SOLUTIONS

39

							24
0	2	3	7	2	3	0	17
8	0	6	9	0	4	9	36
0	1	5	2	4	5	9	26
7	0	2	0	3	3	6	21
9	2	7	8	5	8	3	42
4	3	9	3	4	8	6	37
6	0	7	3	8	9	3	36
34	8	39	32	26	40	36	**21**

40

							35
4	8	0	8	5	8	1	34
2	4	5	8	5	8	4	36
7	1	4	1	4	0	9	26
1	3	1	5	3	9	1	23
7	1	9	3	2	5	4	31
2	2	6	1	8	8	2	29
6	7	7	7	4	0	2	33
29	26	32	33	31	38	23	**29**

41

							12
1	6	1	6	0	7	1	22
5	3	0	1	2	0	6	17
8	1	3	1	0	6	1	20
0	7	1	2	4	9	5	28
1	4	0	9	6	4	9	33
1	3	6	6	4	7	7	34
6	6	8	5	9	1	4	39
22	30	19	30	25	34	33	26

42

							40
2	6	9	5	8	5	8	43
7	0	5	2	2	8	6	30
5	7	1	3	4	2	6	28
7	6	9	1	3	0	6	32
0	9	9	0	9	4	9	40
3	2	6	8	7	4	6	36
8	4	8	1	2	7	9	39
32	34	47	20	35	30	50	26

SOLUTIONS

43

								38
4	2	8	4	4	2	5	1	30
9	4	5	3	9	6	7	6	49
9	7	9	4	6	7	7	5	54
9	5	0	2	7	9	6	6	44
5	9	5	9	1	3	6	9	47
8	8	3	5	4	9	6	0	43
5	4	8	1	4	8	5	8	43
0	2	0	1	9	9	5	1	27
49	41	38	29	44	53	47	36	35

44

								24
3	8	5	9	0	8	4	1	38
5	5	1	9	5	7	3	4	39
7	5	8	8	4	5	3	4	44
6	5	3	6	2	2	8	5	37
1	3	3	1	3	7	6	6	30
5	7	7	1	5	1	3	0	29
1	0	6	9	2	4	2	2	26
5	1	8	7	7	8	8	8	52
33	34	41	50	28	42	37	30	36

SOLUTIONS

45

								26
0	3	5	2	8	4	5	8	35
9	1	3	8	5	4	1	4	35
2	7	2	6	8	1	3	4	33
9	1	3	8	1	4	6	6	38
8	8	9	5	6	8	8	1	53
9	8	3	7	0	9	7	2	45
8	0	8	0	7	9	8	6	46
7	3	5	6	5	9	5	5	45
52	31	38	42	40	48	43	36	39

46

								22
3	2	8	3	2	8	9	1	36
4	8	9	9	9	2	1	0	42
9	2	3	2	1	5	1	0	23
7	0	7	9	0	5	2	9	39
1	8	6	1	4	7	9	1	37
4	6	5	2	9	3	1	8	38
5	8	1	7	7	3	7	1	39
1	9	1	2	7	2	9	3	34
34	43	40	35	39	35	39	23	40

47

								36
5	1	1	2	2	1	0	1	13
5	1	3	9	5	2	7	1	33
6	7	9	4	6	2	3	0	37
8	6	0	4	6	3	7	1	35
2	3	1	1	4	1	2	7	21
9	6	4	3	8	5	4	0	39
0	7	4	1	7	0	0	7	26
8	0	5	8	1	8	1	2	33
43	31	27	32	39	22	24	19	30

48

								42
9	2	1	9	8	6	5	8	48
4	8	8	3	7	9	6	9	54
3	2	0	0	2	4	9	1	21
4	4	6	7	7	3	0	1	32
3	3	0	3	7	1	9	5	31
2	6	6	5	2	8	6	5	40
1	1	9	4	9	4	4	8	40
7	0	2	5	8	2	3	3	30
33	26	32	36	50	37	42	40	46

SOLUTIONS

49

								14
4	7	0	4	5	5	2	3	30
4	5	6	9	4	5	3	5	41
3	2	4	5	9	0	6	7	36
9	9	7	3	0	3	0	1	32
9	1	7	3	8	7	7	9	51
3	9	4	0	9	6	1	7	39
9	1	5	5	1	5	0	7	33
0	3	1	2	9	9	2	6	32
41	37	34	31	45	40	21	45	36

50

									45
1	7	8	3	0	5	9	4	8	45
8	5	2	3	2	1	7	9	2	39
9	7	2	9	3	2	5	9	4	50
7	7	8	2	5	7	5	2	5	48
3	8	6	2	4	3	7	9	7	49
8	5	8	0	0	4	9	4	1	39
6	0	8	1	1	2	5	6	1	30
0	3	2	7	6	2	8	1	6	35
1	1	3	2	7	6	9	6	6	41
43	43	47	29	28	32	64	50	40	30

51

									39
0	8	4	3	9	8	9	5	4	50
1	4	4	0	4	2	9	8	2	34
2	7	6	7	6	2	9	9	0	48
8	8	0	1	5	2	7	7	2	40
1	1	1	3	2	5	6	0	3	22
6	8	2	8	3	8	6	3	3	47
6	1	0	7	7	8	4	0	6	39
1	1	4	2	2	6	8	6	3	33
5	0	3	4	8	3	7	1	5	36
30	38	24	35	46	44	65	39	28	36

52

									33
2	3	3	1	9	5	0	0	2	25
8	8	4	6	2	6	0	7	7	48
1	0	4	0	5	2	4	2	5	23
6	4	7	5	2	3	1	5	0	33
8	9	3	6	2	4	7	8	8	55
0	9	6	7	7	7	9	2	6	53
4	9	2	2	8	9	3	9	8	54
4	1	4	6	4	7	8	1	2	37
5	6	3	2	3	7	7	3	7	43
38	49	36	35	42	50	39	37	45	39

53

									36
8	8	7	1	9	0	7	7	6	53
4	2	2	7	2	3	1	4	0	25
7	8	4	7	0	1	3	5	5	40
7	0	6	4	7	1	8	7	0	40
6	9	0	8	6	1	2	0	3	35
2	9	2	2	6	4	0	8	7	40
8	6	3	6	6	3	4	8	1	45
6	9	3	1	5	6	1	5	9	45
2	9	0	1	2	4	3	6	9	36
50	60	27	37	43	23	29	50	40	46

54

									36
6	2	0	6	7	5	1	0	5	32
6	4	7	4	5	3	2	4	5	40
5	5	1	7	6	0	1	6	7	38
1	6	4	0	7	7	8	4	6	43
5	4	1	1	0	6	9	6	6	38
7	9	7	5	4	0	4	6	6	48
2	1	4	8	2	8	2	3	1	31
6	3	6	6	5	6	0	3	0	35
7	4	3	8	1	6	4	5	7	45
45	38	33	45	37	41	31	37	43	23

SOLUTIONS

55

									45
1	6	2	6	4	5	1	8	8	41
6	2	6	1	9	9	1	4	8	46
0	2	9	7	5	9	4	2	8	46
5	4	0	6	8	7	3	3	2	38
7	3	2	7	1	7	2	7	0	36
4	9	1	5	7	5	5	8	2	46
3	1	5	0	4	2	2	5	7	29
2	9	4	2	2	3	9	4	7	42
2	0	4	7	9	0	7	2	8	39
30	36	33	41	49	47	34	43	50	38

56

									42
2	8	5	4	4	1	6	7	0	37
8	9	9	5	2	4	5	5	8	55
3	4	9	4	1	1	6	4	4	36
0	8	8	8	5	3	0	6	1	39
0	8	8	8	0	7	7	5	6	49
4	3	0	3	3	3	7	8	8	39
8	4	8	3	0	7	0	4	4	38
4	9	0	2	0	0	6	3	0	24
8	3	4	2	9	6	8	9	3	52
37	56	51	39	24	32	45	51	34	37

57

										47
7	4	1	3	4	0	6	9	1	5	40
5	7	8	4	4	6	2	2	9	7	54
1	1	8	0	1	4	2	5	1	0	23
5	9	2	7	1	7	8	1	9	4	53
1	5	8	6	4	9	7	5	8	6	59
9	3	3	8	6	4	2	6	5	1	47
5	6	3	0	8	6	4	6	0	3	41
6	3	0	3	0	1	2	8	8	4	35
9	2	6	8	3	4	0	9	3	4	48
3	7	0	6	1	9	8	5	5	3	47
51	47	39	45	32	50	41	56	49	37	55

58

										27
8	6	3	4	4	0	6	4	3	4	42
7	4	1	5	1	2	6	4	3	0	33
2	7	4	7	3	9	7	3	2	2	46
5	3	3	1	5	3	7	7	3	6	43
9	6	6	4	5	0	2	6	8	5	51
0	3	0	8	1	5	1	9	0	4	31
5	1	9	2	6	1	3	3	0	1	31
8	1	1	7	8	3	0	1	2	2	33
4	6	6	3	4	1	5	3	8	0	40
0	0	8	4	8	1	4	1	9	3	38
48	37	41	45	45	25	41	41	38	27	42

SOLUTIONS

59

										31
4	5	5	8	0	6	9	9	6	4	56
1	4	0	0	4	4	7	9	2	2	33
8	1	8	0	8	8	9	4	3	3	52
5	8	0	2	9	7	0	6	5	4	46
3	3	8	1	1	2	6	9	8	3	44
9	3	4	4	2	3	8	4	6	9	52
0	8	6	8	8	9	2	2	4	5	52
3	7	1	8	7	2	5	6	7	7	53
7	8	1	4	4	2	1	7	4	6	44
0	6	6	7	2	9	6	4	3	7	50
40	53	39	42	45	52	53	60	48	50	41

60

										50
7	1	0	1	6	3	2	3	4	2	29
8	4	3	9	2	0	8	5	5	7	51
8	3	3	7	6	4	1	8	7	1	48
4	1	3	1	4	9	1	1	1	8	33
1	9	3	8	9	2	5	8	4	5	54
5	3	7	3	8	3	8	5	6	3	51
6	1	0	6	4	2	5	5	7	7	43
4	8	7	2	0	2	3	5	4	9	44
6	9	8	4	9	8	9	1	5	6	65
2	2	3	6	4	9	0	9	8	6	49
51	41	37	47	52	42	42	50	51	54	48

61

										56
1	2	3	0	5	8	6	9	6	7	47
8	8	4	3	6	9	2	4	5	1	50
5	4	3	5	9	9	2	9	0	4	50
8	8	5	3	9	1	9	9	5	5	62
7	6	1	3	3	0	7	7	3	9	46
2	7	1	0	6	1	6	4	6	1	34
8	3	2	2	5	3	7	1	5	5	41
1	7	3	4	3	7	6	0	6	4	41
9	6	9	8	4	3	9	7	2	8	65
9	0	1	2	7	5	4	3	2	4	37
58	51	32	30	57	46	58	53	40	48	32

62

										38
9	8	0	6	1	3	5	2	0	7	41
2	7	5	4	2	2	6	6	4	7	45
2	4	3	4	1	2	1	1	7	0	25
4	3	0	5	0	2	7	9	8	2	40
8	8	8	7	3	1	7	4	7	9	62
8	3	9	9	9	2	8	9	0	5	62
4	9	8	1	2	4	9	0	8	0	45
9	7	2	5	4	2	7	4	0	1	41
5	3	2	9	7	1	8	3	7	3	48
3	6	7	4	6	1	1	5	9	2	44
54	58	44	54	35	20	59	43	50	36	51

SOLUTIONS

63

										50
2	7	1	5	2	5	5	1	0	7	35
3	7	8	0	2	0	0	6	8	9	43
0	4	3	8	8	3	1	6	1	7	41
5	9	4	0	7	2	1	1	4	6	39
3	9	3	4	2	3	1	8	2	7	42
8	9	3	9	5	0	0	3	5	7	49
4	1	2	3	4	8	0	3	8	4	37
7	8	0	6	4	5	4	1	3	2	40
5	8	6	5	7	3	6	2	6	3	51
9	1	6	7	9	2	7	1	1	8	51
46	63	36	47	50	31	25	32	38	60	29

Name: ___________________________________

Age: ___________________________________

Notes

Name: ______________________________

Age: ______________________________

Notes

____

____

____

____

____

____

____

____

____

____

Also Available by the Same Authors:

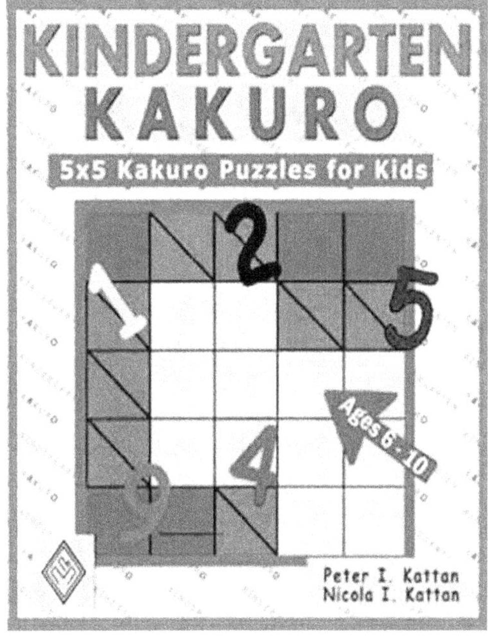

Math Puzzles for Kids 2
Number Blocks for Children

9 798869 210548